Power

LIVING BY THE SPIRIT OF GOD

Scott Nelson

Foreword by Alan Hirsch

FORGE GUIDES FOR MISSIONAL CONVERSATION

IVP Connect

An imprint of InterVarsity Press
Downers Grove, Illinois

InterVarsity Press
P.O. Box 1400, Downers Grove, IL 60515-1426
World Wide Web: www.ivpress.com
E-mail: email@ivpress.com

InterVarsity Press® is the book-publishing division of InterVarsity Christian Fellowship/USA®, a movement
of students and faculty active on campus at hundreds of universities, colleges and schools of nursing in the
United States of America, and a member movement of the International Fellowship of Evangelical Students.
For information about local and regional activities, write Public Relations Dept., InterVarsity Christian
Fellowship/USA, 6400 Schroeder Rd., P.O. Box 7895, Madison, WI 53707-7895, or visit the IVCF website at
<www.intervarsity.org>.

All Scripture quotations, unless otherwise indicated, are taken from the Holy Bible, New International
Version®, NIV® Copyright © 1973, 1978, 1984, 2011 by Biblica, Inc.™ Used by permission. All rights
reserved worldwide.

While all stories in this book are true, some names and identifying information in this book have been
changed to protect the privacy of the individuals involved.

Cover design: Cindy Kiple
Interior design: Beth Hagenberg

Images: © Jay Graygor/iStockphoto

ISBN 978-0-8308-1046-8 (print)
ISBN 978-0-8308-9573-1 (digital)

Printed in the United States of America ∞

Library of Congress Cataloging-in-Publication Data
A catalog record for this book is available from the Library of Congress.

| P | 20 | 19 | 18 | 17 | 16 | 15 | 14 | 13 | 12 | 11 | 10 | 9 | 8 | 7 | 6 | 5 | 4 | 3 | 2 | 1 |
| Y | 30 | 29 | 28 | 27 | 26 | 25 | 24 | 23 | 22 | 21 | 20 | 19 | 18 | 17 | 16 | 15 | 14 | 13 |

CONTENTS

FOREWORD

For the better part of two decades now, *missional* has been equal
parts buzzword and byword in the contemporary church.

Many church leaders have decried the trendiness of the term, pre-
dicting that it will eventually go the way of all fads, and that responsible church leadership involves simply waiting it out, keeping the
faith. And it's hard to deny the trendiness of the term: as the editors
of *Leadership Journal* noted in their preface to an article of mine five
years ago, "A quick search on Google uncovers the presence of 'missional communities,' 'missional leaders,' 'missional worship,' even
'missional seating,' and 'missional coffee.'"[1] The closer the application
of the term approaches absurdity, the less seriously we are inclined to
take it.

And yet over the same period the concept of a missional church has
proved its durability. Conference after conference has organized itself
around the concept that God is on mission in the world, and that as
means to the end of achieving his mission God has created a church.
Seminary after seminary has reconfigured its core curricula to take
the model of a church on mission seriously, and to train pastors and
other leaders to understand themselves as missionaries first, "keepers"
of the faith a distant second. What so many have dismissed as a fad or

a trend, substantial and growing numbers of people are recognizing as a paradigm shift.

Of course, any number of paradigm-shifting conversations are taking place at the conceptual level among the leadership of the global church at any given moment. Many such conversations bubble up only to dissipate; such in-house deliberation is part of the long history of the faith. It is in this historical reality that the durability and trajectory of the missional church conversation reveals its significance. More than a mere theoretical conversation, the missional church bears the marks of a true movement—broad-based, but with a cohesive sense of self-understanding; goal-driven, but deeply rooted in principles and conviction; critical of the status quo, yet always motivated by the greater good. Christianity itself has always been a movement, inspired by the God who created the world and called it good, who so loved the world that he gave his only Son for it.

Any movement over time has the capacity to atrophy, to be distracted by its own sense of self-preservation, to be enthralled by the beauty of its past accomplishments and the currency of its cultural power. But the original vision of the movement relentlessly beckons, confronting our self-congratulation and propelling us toward the greater good of our original calling.

At Forge we have always said that the best critique of the bad is the practice of the better. With this series of guides on missional practices we are trying to help create a more productive and better future for a church now in systemic decline. We believe the church was made for far more than mere self-preservation, and certainly not for retreat. We were made to be a highly transformative Jesus movement; we had best get on with being that. To do this we need to redisciple the church into its calling and mission. Discipleship is a huge key, and for this we need tools.

Every movement requires the education—the *formation*—of its people. I believe the next phase of the movement that is the missional church resides not so much in seminaries or elder meetings as around the tables of people of faith wherever they find themselves. These Forge Guides for Missional Conversation are intended to facilitate those conversations—to help you, wherever you are, to step together into the flow of God's mission in the world.

Scott Nelson is particularly equipped to facilitate such conversations. He has held leadership positions in traditional churches and studied the church's mission while pursuing his doctorate. He has taken on the responsibility of the theological direction of Forge Mission Training Network in America even as he has developed a missional community in the neighborhood where he lives. The mission of God is thoroughly integrated into Scott's life—heart and soul, mind and strength—which is as it is intended to be.

Each of the five guides that make up this series will be valuable on its own; thoroughly scriptural, accessibly theological, highly practical and fundamentally spiritual, each will give you a fuller appreciation of what it means to be a follower of Jesus on God's mission. Taken together, however, they are a sort of curriculum for a movement: you and your friends will be fully equipped for every good work that God has in mind for you in the place where you find yourself.

Our missionary God created a church in service to his mission. We were made for a movement. Read on if you're ready to move!

Alan Hirsch

INTRODUCTION
TO THE FORGE GUIDES

I've been obsessed with the idea of helping Christians develop a missionary imagination for their daily lives ever since I began to develop such an imagination back in 2007. My missionary imagination began at a church staff retreat. I was asked what I thought our church staff should do if God dropped us all from a helicopter into our city with absolutely no resources and asked us to start a church. While thinking of my answer to this question, I realized I would have to take on the mindset of a missionary—go out to the people, learn who they are, get involved in their lives, care about what they care about. The years that have passed since that fateful question have been an amazing journey for me. I quit my job, dove into full-time study of the missionary mindset in Christian congregations, began exploring ways to live like a missionary in the condominium complex where my wife and I currently live, and teamed up with the Forge America Mission Training Network to be a part of an organization that actively seeks to implant a missionary mindset in Christians and their faith communities.

I've written these guides to help you ask some of the same questions that I asked, and to help you think about what it might look like if you, your group or your church were to develop a missionary imagination for everyday living. There are at least three reasons why it is crucially important that you ask these questions and develop a missionary imagination.

The first reason is the cultural changes that are taking place in Western contexts. Changes such as increasing globalization, religious and cultural pluralism, huge advances in science and technology, the collapse of many modern principles and the growth of postmodernism, and the secularization of the West have drastically altered many cultural landscapes. If the gospel is to be proclaimed faithfully and effectively in these changing contexts, Christians must be missionaries who study cultures in order to translate the gospel so that all can clearly hear it. Simply saying and doing the same things in the same ways as generations past is no longer effective.

A second reason it is vitally important for Christians to develop a missionary mindset is the crisis facing the institutional church. The many different statistical studies that measure the size and influence of the church in the United States are sobering. Despite the explosion of megachurches, congregations in the United States as a whole consist of older people and fewer participants, and experience decreased influence in local contexts. The institutional, established church is experiencing a serious internal crisis as contexts change and congregations fail to adapt. Christians must regain a sense of their missionary calling if the trend of a diminishing role for the Christian faith is to be reversed in the West.

Third, I see evidence of a common longing for a deeper, lived-out faith among many Christians, especially among emerging generations. I've felt it and so have many others who I have read and talked with. It is the feeling that something about the way I am participating in church and faith seems to be missing; it seems to be too easy or too shallow. Conversations with Christians across the country reveal a longing to be challenged, to do something significant with their faith, to make a difference in the lives of people both globally and locally. By developing a missionary imagination for everyday living, these Christians develop a mindset that can lead to deeper expressions of faith, which ultimately reorient a person's whole life around what God is doing and wants to do in this world.

My life story and the three reasons I just listed compelled me to write and use these conversation guides for my own small group. Perhaps you have had a similar experience, or maybe one of the three reasons prompted you to pick up the guides. Even if not, I sincerely hope the questions contained in these guides will infect your minds, as they did mine. And I sincerely hope the mission of God will infect your lives, as I pray every day for it to infect mine.

USING THE FORGE GUIDES

My focus in creating these guides has not been to give you all the answers. I firmly believe you and the members of your group need to discern the answers for yourselves, and further, to generate the creativity that will shape your imagination for what a missionary lifestyle might look like in your life and community. My task in creating these guides is to help you ask good questions.

While creating these guides, I kept coming back to the idea of minimalist running shoes. The science behind these increasingly popular shoes claims that the human body is naturally equipped to run. Big, cushiony, fancy running shoes are not only unnecessary but counterproductive. What runners really need is a simple shoe that accentuates their natural abilities, encourages proper running form and protects their feet from environmental hazards.

These guides are designed to be a lot like minimalist running shoes. They offer the bare minimum you will need to ask good questions, seek innovative answers and develop a new imagination. The guides do not do the work for you. Rather, let them draw out your natural ability to hear from Scripture, to think about the world around you, to wonder about who God is and to imagine ways you can live as a missionary.

These four practices appear in each lesson under the headings

"Dwelling in the Word," "Contextual Analysis," "Theological Reflection" and "Missionary Imagination." I have identified relevant biblical texts, but it is your job to listen for how God is speaking to you and your group. The guides also provide probing questions about your local context, but it is your job to do the analysis required to provide the answers. Similarly, the guides will provide theological content and point to basic principles of missional living, but it is your job to reflect on the nature of God and how he is asking you to live out his mission in your context.

To help you understand what you will be doing as you work through the conversation guides, a brief description of each basic practice follows. Please note that some groups will naturally gravitate to some of the practices more than to others. Don't feel the need to go through each section with a fine-toothed comb. There is more material than will likely be needed for most group gatherings, so be flexible with the practices and allow the group to choose how much time to allocate to each section.

Practice 1: Dwelling in the Word

Each group gathering begins with a time to hear from Scripture through communal reading and listening.[2] Dwelling in the same text over a period of six weeks (or more!) will allow your group to begin developing a shared imagination and a shared openness to the many things God may want to say and do through the text.

The group listens to the passage, reflects in silence for a few moments and then breaks into pairs to discuss two questions about the text. After sufficient time has passed (while allowing adequate time for the remainder of the session), the group gathers together. Individuals share what their partners heard in the text while answers are recorded. This section concludes with the group asking, What might God be up to in this passage for us today?

Sometimes people will doubt the value of returning to the same text time after time, but trust the process and believe that the Bible is the living Word of God. The more you continue to return to the same text, the more you will find blessing at the insight you gain, the habits you learn, the imagination you develop and the community you form.

One final point can help you get started on the right foot: dwelling in the Word is about hearing from God's Word and hearing from each other. Each person is responsible for helping one other person give voice to what she or he heard from the text and to then be an advocate for that person's thoughts in the larger group. These practices are intended to help the group create an environment where thoughts are safely shared and members listen deeply to one another. Over time, dwelling in the Word is a powerful tool that can form a community of the Spirit where the presence and power of the Spirit is both welcome and expected.

Practice 2: Contextual Analysis

Missionaries know that the gospel must be translated—literally and figuratively—into local contexts. Every local culture is unique and will hear and receive the gospel in different ways. A good missionary learns to understand local cultures so that he or she can inculturate the gospel in a way specifically tailored to a specific people group. At times of inculturation into new contexts, the gospel has proven to be the most effective at bringing about radical transformation in individuals, communities and whole societies. The Forge Guides for Missional Conversation are designed to help Christian communities inculturate and translate the gospel into their local contexts by facilitating shared practices of contextual analysis during group gatherings.

Practices of contextual analysis will focus on three main areas: describing the local context, discerning what God is already doing in the local context and wondering together what God might want to do in the local context. A variety of ways to practice contextual analysis are provided in each session. Sometimes the group will simply have questions to answer. At other times they will be asked to complete an activity or reflect personally. It is hoped that the variety of practices provided will lead the group to a new understanding of their context and will help the group faithfully proclaim and live out the gospel in new and exciting ways that transform the members of the group and the world around them.

Practice 3: Theological Reflection

David Kelsey defines theology as the search to understand and know God truly.[3] Theology in this sense becomes wisdom in relationship to God. Much like understanding an instruction manual about building a bike leads to the ability to build that bike, searching to understand God brings about some ability to relate with God through spiritual practices, worship and faith. Those who know God can sense and participate in what God is doing in the world around them.

The section on theological reflection is designed to help your group seek to know God truly so that the group might become wise in relationship to God. It will encourage you to actively wonder about who God is and what he is up to in the world. Scripture passages and a few reflection questions will be provided for the group to study. Sometimes other sources of theological reflection—such as distinct church traditions, church history or other texts—will be provided. No matter what specific content is provided for you to reflect on, the goal will always be the same and that is for your group to ask, What can we know about who God is and what God does? How does this influence the way we relate to God and join with him in what he is doing?

Practice 4: Missionary Imagination

Each session will conclude with a time for developing a missionary imagination through conversation, personal reflection, group affirmation, prayer or a variety of other activities. The time set aside for missionary imagination is intended to help each individual in the group gain a better sense of his or her own missionary calling, and also to help the group as a whole develop a missionary imagination for its existence. I've tried particularly hard to provide a wide variety of activities in this section. The goal of these activities as well as their very nature is meant to help you and your group break the mold when it comes to calling, vision and imagination. When my own small group went through this material, we had a blast doing things like drawing pictures, sharing stories, writing limericks and making collages, as well as answering the more conventional discussion questions. Have fun with this section and do your best to encourage one another to be imaginative, innovative and experimental in missionary living.

Before We Meet Again

Midweek assignments are given at the end of each week's session. These assignments are fun little projects designed to help group members continue to think about the session throughout the week. For instance, one assignment might ask members to take pictures of three things during the week that they think represent the work of God in the world. Time for the group to review the midweek assignment is often built into the next week's session. I strongly encourage your group to complete these assignments whenever possible. My own group really enjoyed them!

Recording and Reflecting

As your group talks through these guides, my final recommendation is to take notes during the discussions, whether individually or through a general secretary. These records will help you discern patterns and commonalities that may help you see what God is doing in your lives.

INTRODUCTION

Power: Living by the Spirit of God

I was sitting at a campfire with our small group when I said to the guy next to me, "I've always wished I was a Pentecostal."

He quickly responded with a derogatory "Why?"

My reply to him was simple: "Because they actually believe in the Holy Spirit."

The tradition my friend and I come from tends to be a bit uptight. Still, my friend retorted, he certainly believed in the Holy Spirit. But when I asked him when was the last time he had talked about the Spirit of God leading, equipping or speaking to him, he admitted he couldn't think of a time.

For much of my life I was content with a mere passing knowledge of the work of the Spirit. Once I began to view myself as a missionary to my neighbors, however, I found myself wanting to know more about the work of the Spirit and the way the Spirit could empower me to live out God's mission in my everyday life. I guess you could say that once I actively tried to work for God's mission, I wanted to know more about the tools God had given me to faithfully accomplish that mission.

This study guide grew out of my own path to develop an imagination for how God's Spirit might work through his people today.

Two authors, Michael Welker and Craig Van Gelder, shaped my journey and therefore this guide. Their writing helped me think of the Spirit as God's power at work in and through God's people to accomplish God's purposes. Studying the Spirit, I see that God's power works in his people by liberating them from sin and equipping them with gifts that reveal God's grace to the world. I have found this understanding to be greatly encouraging, helping me live boldly as a missionary. I hope and pray it will be encouraging to you and your group as well, and will aid you in your journey to develop a missionary imagination for your everyday life.

LIVING BY THE POWER
THAT GUARANTEES THE FUTURE

There is a brilliant little story tucked away in 2 Chronicles 20. As the story opens, God's people are in peril. They call on God to help them. God answers their cry for help by sending his Spirit to empower a lone man to speak. That man delivers a message of hope to the people, telling them not to fear for God is with them and will fight on their behalf. Encouraged by the message, the people respond with worship and obedience as they watch God win a victory for them.

The goal for this week's session is for you to consider that the Spirit of God is the power of God to guarantee the future for his people. Understanding this allows you to respond in worship and obedience as you watch God win the victory all around you. Throughout today's conversation, continually ask yourself what future God is guaranteeing you, and how you ought to respond to that guarantee.

Dwelling in the Word

- Begin in prayer, inviting the Spirit to guide your group as you dwell in the text.

- Read aloud Romans 8:1-17.

- After the reading has been completed, allow a few moments of silence to reflect on the passage and what stands out to you.

- Break into pairs (preferably with someone you don't know well) and discuss the following questions. Use this time to practice listening to each other as well as to the text.

  - What in the text captured your imagination?

  - What question would you most like to ask a biblical scholar?

- Gather once again as a large group and share your partners' responses.

- Review these responses and discuss: What might God be up to in the passage for us today?

Contextual Analysis

1. Read 2 Chronicles 20. The story took place in a specific location at a specific time. Describe the specific location around you. What are the people like? How would you describe this time in history?

2. God's people were being threatened with destruction in 2 Chronicles 20. Obviously, if God's people were destroyed, they could not fulfill their God-given mission to be a blessing to the nations

around them. What powers or forces in your local context threaten to keep God's people from living out their mission to be a blessing?

3. God responds to his people's plight in the story by encouraging his people and defeating the opposing forces through the power of his Spirit. How do you see God's Spirit working in the world around you? In what ways would you say God is fighting against forces that try to keep God's mission from being achieved?

4. The story in 2 Chronicles 20 concludes with God's people worshiping him, the foreign nations fearing God for his mighty acts on behalf of his people, and the realization of peace and security for God's people. God's purposes, in a sense, had been accomplished. What would it look like for God to accomplish his purposes in your local context?

Theological Reflection: *The Spirit Who Guarantees the Future*

5. Second Chronicles 20 is not the only place in the Bible where

God's Spirit is revealed as a power that guarantees the future for God's people. Romans 5:1-5 claims that our hope in God does not disappoint us, because we have been given the Holy Spirit. Read the text as a group and try to write a one-sentence summary of the point Paul is making. Look at the surrounding context of verses 1-5 if you need to in order to write your summary.

6. Break into pairs and read one of the following passages, answer the corresponding question, then report back to the group.

   • 2 Corinthians 1:22: The author calls the Spirit a deposit and a guarantee (*deposit* can also be translated "down payment," "first installment" or "pledge"). What do you think the author means by saying the Spirit is a *deposit* that guarantees what is to come?

   • 2 Corinthians 5:1-10: The same Greek word used to call the Spirit a "deposit" in 2 Corinthians 1:22 appears in 2 Corinthians 5:5. What point is the author making about the Spirit here? How are the people to respond to the idea that the Spirit is a guarantee?

- Ephesians 1:3-14: What point is the author making about the Spirit here? How are the people to respond to the idea that the Spirit is a guarantee?

7. Considering these three texts, write one sentence that describes how the Holy Spirit is a guarantee or down payment. Write a second sentence that describes how God's people should live in light of the truth of the Spirit as a guarantee of the future.

Missionary Imagination

The texts considered during the conversation this week reveal how the Spirit liberates people from fear, doubt or insecurity by guaranteeing their future. The Israelites heard a message through the power of the Spirit in 2 Chronicles 20 that convinced them their future was guaranteed since the power of God's Spirit was with them. They responded to this message by worshiping God in confidence and obeying his somewhat crazy command for them to do nothing while their enemies gathered around them. The author of 2 Corinthians says that Christians are always full of courage because they know that the Spirit is the guarantee of their future.

Liberating God's people from fear by guaranteeing their future is an essential part of the Spirit's work, which may be summarized in these two statements:

- The primary work of the Spirit of God is to empower the people of God to participate in the mission of God and in so doing to contribute to the glory of God.

- The primary means by which the Spirit empowers God's people is by liberating them from their sinful lives and equipping them with gifts to reveal God's grace to the world.

8. Get into groups of 2-3 and discuss fears, insecurities or doubts that might keep you from living as boldly as you ought to as missionaries for God.

9. Once everyone in your group of 2-3 has had a chance to share, pray over one another, asking God to free you from all fear and doubt, and to give you hope in light of the guaranteed future ahead of you.

Before We Meet Again

- Continue to read and reflect upon Romans 8:1-17, 2 Chronicles 20 or any other passage from this week's conversation. Record your thoughts here:

- Rewrite 2 Chronicles 20 as a personal story with you or your group taking the place of the Israelites. The story can be a true story from the past or a hypothetical situation in the future. Follow the pattern of the biblical story (threat, prayer to God, God's response, worship and obedience, God's faithfulness). Be prepared to share your story at the beginning of your next group meeting.

- Write the two summary statements about the work of the Spirit from the end of session 1 on a note card. Place this card where you will see it often.

- Write one sentence that summarizes your current understanding of what it looks like to live by the power of the Spirit.

LIVING BY THE POWER
THAT CONQUERS DEATH

One of the most significant images of the Spirit found in the Bible is the description of the Spirit being poured out from heaven. Heaven is described in Scripture as the realm of God that is inaccessible to humans, but which exerts influence over life on earth. Sometimes God's wrath is poured out of heaven because of the sinful ways of the people of earth. In such cases, the imagery includes destructive forces like floods, fires or torrential rains. In contrast, when God's Spirit is poured out, the imagery is that of a perfectly gentle rain falling on desperately dry and thirsty land. "The Spirit of God acts in the same way as the rain, which, coming down from heaven, enables an entire landscape with the most varied living beings to burst into new life together, full of freshness and vitality."[4]

Those who live on mission for God through the power of the Spirit will serve as much-needed rain to a thirsty world. This truth is the topic of this week's conversation.

Begin by sharing your 2 Chronicles 20 story rewrites. Spend a few minutes discussing your observations once everyone in the group has shared their stories. Did you notice any common themes? Key differences? Vivid pictures that have sparked your imagination?

Dwelling in the Word

- Begin in prayer, inviting the Spirit to guide your group as you dwell in the text.

- Read aloud Romans 8:1-17.

- After the reading has been completed, allow a few moments of silence to reflect on the passage and what stands out to you.

- Break into pairs (preferably with someone you don't know well) and discuss the following questions. Use this time to practice listening to each other as well as to the text.

  - What in the text captured your imagination?

  - What question would you most like to ask a biblical scholar?

- Gather once again as a large group and share your partners' responses.

- Review these responses and discuss: What might God be up to in the passage for us today?

Contextual Analysis

The Spirit of God is like rain that brings life and vitality to you, your group and the world around you.

1. What in your context would you describe as dry and thirsty land?

2. What might it look like for the Spirit of God to be poured out on these dry areas?

3. Think of a specific person in your local context to whom you feel God has sent you. What might it look like for the Spirit of God to be poured out on the dry places in this person's life?

Theological Reflection: *The Spirit Who Brings to Life That Which Was Once Dead*

4. Read Isaiah 32:9-20, noting the imagery of the Spirit being poured out in verse 15. What was dead about the land before the rain of the Spirit came? What kind of life did the Spirit bring?

5. Break into pairs and read one of the following texts: Isaiah 44:3; Ezekiel 39:29; Joel 2:28-29; Acts 2:17-18; 10:45; Romans 5:5; Titus 3:5-6. In what way(s) does the Spirit bring life to that which was dead?

6. Read Ezekiel 47:1-12 and John 7:37-39. Jesus equates the Holy Spirit with rivers of living water. Assume, then, that the river in Ezekiel 47 represents the powerful results of the work of the Spirit. What effect does the river have on the surrounding world in Ezekiel 47? How might this relate to the Spirit?

Missionary Imagination

Remember these statements from session 1.

- The primary work of the Spirit of God is to empower the people of God to participate in the mission of God and in so doing to contribute to the glory of God.

- The primary means by which the Spirit empowers God's people is by liberating them from their sinful lives and equipping them with gifts to reveal God's grace to the world.

Many of the passages that describe the Spirit of God being poured out specify a pouring out in the lives of people. While God is surely capable of pouring out the life-giving Spirit directly into a context, God seems most often to intentionally work by the Spirit through his people.

7. Brainstorm what it would look like for you as individuals or as a group to be the means by which God's Spirit brings life to your surrounding world. Tell another person in your group how you can imagine the Spirit working through him or her to bless another.

8. Think about a rain dance. Rain dances consist of rhythms, patterns, rituals and movements meant to invoke rain—they are an *invitation* for rain. What rhythms, patterns and rituals of life could you develop individually and as a group to invite the rain of the Spirit to the dry places around you?

9. Based on your answer to the previous question, identify practical next steps you can take to adopt the rhythms, patterns and rituals of a Spirit-powered missionary.

Before We Meet Again

- Continue to read and reflect on Romans 8:1-17, Ezekiel 47 or any other passage from this week's conversation. Record your thoughts here:

- Look at the two summary statements about the work of the Spirit. Rewrite them on a note card using different colored markers or pencils for each phrase or clause.

- Pretend that you are a weather reporter for your area, but the weather system you are reporting on is the rain of the Spirit. Prepare some kind of presentation (newspaper article, news video, live presentation, etc.) that describes the new weather pattern and the effect it is having on the local environment. Be prepared to share your presentation at your next meeting.

- Based on your continued conversations and reflections, modify your one-sentence summary of your current understanding of what it looks like to live by the power of the Spirit (look back to your sentence from the end of session 1). Record your new sentence here.

LIVING BY THE POWER
THAT MAKES GOD KNOWN

I was spending some time in prayer and fasting shortly before proposing to my future wife, Andrea, when I came to an important conclusion about the nature of marriage. I realized that at its core marriage is a relationship that uniquely shows the world what God's love looks like. I asked myself, *Is Andrea a woman who could love me and be loved by me in such a way that the world would see God's love through us?* I knew that she was indeed such a woman. Of course, it took me four more months to plan an adequate proposal, but five years into our marriage our goal has not changed: we still seek to love each other in such a way that God's love is revealed to the world.

I've since extended my principle belief about marriage to all my relationships. The way that I live on mission for God ought to show the world God's love. When someone witnesses my life, my hope is that somewhere in what I do and how I live they might see God and know him for the God he truly is. This principle, I believe, is at the heart of what it looks like to have a missionary imagination for everyday living. The Spirit of God works through his people to make God known to the world.

Begin today's conversation by sharing your weather-report presentations. When you consider your descriptions of the effects of the Spirit on your area, what do you notice? Are there any common threads?

Dwelling in the Word

- Begin in prayer, inviting the Spirit to guide your group as you dwell in the text.

- Read aloud Romans 8:1-17.

- After the reading has been completed, allow a few moments of silence to reflect on the passage and what stands out to you.

- Break into pairs (preferably with someone you don't know well) and discuss the following questions. Use this time to practice listening to each other as well as to the text.

  - What in the text captured your imagination?

  - What question would you most like to ask a biblical scholar?

- Gather once again as a large group and share your partners' responses.

- Review these responses and discuss: What might God be up to in the passage for us today?

Contextual Analysis

Ezekiel 36–37 reveals that the nations near Israel were not completely ignorant of Israel's God, but rather had misconceptions about what God was like. Think about the people around you and answer the following questions:

1. What do you think the people around you know about God? If you were to ask them to describe God what do you think they would say?

2. What are some of the misconceptions of God the people around you might have? How do you think they got these ideas?

3. What do you think it would take to help people in your mission context have a more accurate view of God?

Theological Reflection: *The Spirit Who Reveals God to the World*

A survey of the work of the Spirit in the Bible makes clear that one of the Spirit's primary tasks is to make God known throughout the world. When God gives his Spirit to his people, God's will is revealed, his ways are made known, his identity is established, his actions are identified and his future plans are foretold. These actions contribute to the mission of God and bring God glory by making God known to the communities surrounding God's people. The same holds true today. As God reveals himself to us through the Spirit, we reveal him to others through the Spirit.

4. Read Joel 2:28-32. In what ways will the Spirit make God known? What is meant by "the day of the LORD"? How do you think God's Spirit continues to make God known in these ways today?

5. Read Acts 2:1-41. How is this story a fulfillment of Joel 2:28-32? What is made known about God? How does the Spirit work to make God known in this way today?

6. First Corinthians 2:16 says through the Spirit we have the mind of Christ. What does it mean to have the mind of Christ?

Missionary Imagination

7. Our first summary statement about the work of the Spirit says: "The primary work of the Spirit of God is to empower the people of God to participate in the mission of God and in so doing to contribute to the glory of God." Describe the relationship that you see between making God known to the people around you and contributing to God's glory.

8. Our second summary statement says: "The primary means by which the Spirit empowers God's people is by liberating them from their sinful lives and equipping them with gifts to reveal God's grace to the world." Consider your "world." Make a list of the people or groups of people who observe your life on a regular basis (family, friends, coworkers, neighbors, team members, business owners, etc.).

9. Get into groups of 3-4. Write a short skit that illustrates how the life of a person in your group might make God known to someone around you. Some groups should give a positive or successful example. The other groups should try to illustrate a negative or unsuccessful example.

Before We Meet Again

- Spend some time reading through and studying 1 Corinthians 2:6-16. What does the author say about the knowledge of God and the role of the Spirit in such knowledge?

- Continue to read and reflect on 1 Corinthians 2:6-16, Romans 8:1-17 or any passage from this week's conversation. Record your thoughts here:

- Look again at the list of individuals in your life from question 8. Pray, reflect and journal about what each group of people on your list might know about God based on the way you live your life. What things might you do to better reveal God to those people?

- Do your best to have a conversation with 2-3 people this week about what they think about God or Jesus. You might say, "I was wondering if I could ask you a question, but it is kind of personal. Is that okay? Cool, thanks. Would you mind telling me what you think about God (or Jesus)?" Listen to their answer and try to ask clarifying questions to help draw out what they think. Be prepared for them to ask why you want to know. Have ready an honest answer. In the space that follows, record notes or details from any of the conversations you have. Be prepared to share with the group at your next session.

- Based on your continued conversations and reflections, modify your one-sentence summary of your current understanding of what it looks like to live by the power of the Spirit (look back to the assignments from sessions 1 and 2). Record your new sentence here.

LIVING BY THE POWER THAT ESTABLISHES JUSTICE, PEACE AND FREEDOM

My wife and I try to live like missionaries in the small condominium complex we currently call home. When I first moved in, I thought living like a missionary would look like barbecues, dinner parties and game nights. I envisioned myself becoming everyone's best friend in order to earn the right to give witness to Jesus.

It has been six years since I first moved into this building, and I am far from being everyone's best friend. I can probably count on one hand the number of parties or events I have organized that were attended by more than two or three people. While my wife and I are incredibly thankful for the amazing friendship we have developed with one of our neighbors, it is safe to say that our missionary lives have not gone as expected. Instead of playing the role of community organizer, we have become peacemakers, arbitrators and board members. Getting twelve very different people to live peaceably in a rather small building is hard enough—forget getting them to enjoy one another socially. We've had multiple conflicts arise, and we quickly realized the limitations of our conflict-resolving resources. One dispute lasted over two years, evenly dividing our five-member board, with me in the uncomfortable middle trying to make peace.

My understanding of living like a missionary has matured from simply developing friendships and sharing the gospel to seeing the need to fight for peace, justice and freedom. Living on mission, for my wife and me, has included knocking on neighbors' doors to discuss difficult community conflicts, responding to an endless stream of emails, researching condominium laws and procedures, and keeping the peace at contentious association meetings. We've made a lot of mistakes and learned a lot of lessons on the way, but through it all we have come to appreciate the power of God's Spirit in God's people to accomplish justice, peace and freedom.

Share your notes and reflections from the previous weeks' assignments.

Dwelling in the Word

- Begin in prayer, inviting the Spirit to guide your group as you dwell in the text.

- Read aloud Romans 8:1-17.

- After the reading has been completed, allow a few moments of silence to reflect on the passage and what stands out to you.

- Break into pairs (preferably with someone you don't know well) and discuss the following questions. Use this time to practice listening to each other as well as to the text.

  - What in the text captured your imagination?

  - What question would you most like to ask a biblical scholar?

- Gather once again as a large group and share your partners' responses.
- Review these responses and discuss: What might God be up to in the passage for us today?

Contextual Analysis

No matter where you live, it is likely that there are people around you in need of justice, peace and freedom. It is likely that there are groups and individuals who have been marginalized, who are being unfairly treated, who are oppressed or who are embroiled in conflict. If you are at all like me, your life may often be too busy to take notice of these issues, much less do anything about them. Use the following few minutes to start thinking about the issues that might be right around you.

1. Draw three columns on a large piece of paper or poster board. Head the three columns "Justice/Injustice," "Peace/Conflict" and "Freedom/Oppression." Identify as many local issues in each column as you can.

2. Look at your list. Put stars next to the issues that are the most pressing or important. Underline issues that are largely being ignored. Circle issues that affect the most people.

3. Pick one or two issues that received the most marks (stars, circles, underlines) on your lists. What do you think God might want to accomplish in regard to these issues?

Theological Reflection: *The Spirit Who Establishes Justice, Peace and Freedom*

4. Divide into three groups to explore the following passages from Isaiah, which foretell the coming of the Spirit of the Lord to establish justice, peace and freedom. Read each passage carefully, then describe as much as you can about the text. How does the Spirit work? How are justice, peace and freedom pictured? Who will experience these things? Where will these things take place?

• Isaiah 11

• Isaiah 42:1-17

• Isaiah 61

5. Share your notes from Isaiah 11; 42:1-17; 61. What similarities do you notice?

6. How would you summarize this important message from the prophet Isaiah?

Missionary Imagination

7. Without looking back at the previous sessions, try to repeat the two summary statements about the work of the Spirit. Once you have recorded your best group effort, look back and compare your version to the original. What part is the easiest for you to remember? The hardest?

8. Read Acts 6:1-7. Fighting for justice, peace and freedom in the power of the Spirit doesn't necessarily mean undertaking huge, global endeavors. What are small ways your group can work together to establish justice in your local context?

9. Michael Welker wrote the following about communities committed to mercy:

> Mercy—the sensitivity not only to the distress of other persons, but also to systematically disadvantageous arrangements and to unjust differentiation in a community, and the readiness to remove these wrongs—indeed cannot be confined to a circle of persons and to a field of problems that can be defined once and for all. Mercy must always remain open and sensitive to new groups of weak, afflicted, and disadvantaged persons in a community. . . . A community that is obligated to practice mercy thus becomes committed to constant self-change and self-renewal, to self-critical thinking and reorientation.[5]

Analyze your Christian community based on the Welker quote. Do you practice mercy? How might you do more? Are you open to recognize the needs of new groups? How might you be more open?

10. The Spirit of God breaks down forces of oppression and barriers of conflict, and leads freed people into a new solidarity with one another. What would it look like for you or your group to create new solidarity for people in your local context by overcoming oppression and conflict?

Before We Meet Again

• Continue to read and reflect on Isaiah 11; 42; 61; Romans 8:1-17; or any other passage from this week's conversation. Record your thoughts here:

• On a separate piece of paper, draw a picture of what it would look like for justice, peace and freedom to be established in your local context.

• Research issues of justice, peace and freedom in your local community. Access local news coverage, talk to community leaders, religious leaders or school officials, walk or drive through local neighborhoods, or simply ask people around you about issues important to them. Report your findings here and be prepared to share them with the group at the next meeting:

- Based on your continued conversations and reflections, modify your one-sentence summary of your current understanding of what it looks like to live by the power of the Spirit. Record your new sentence here.

LIVING BY THE POWER THAT
GENERATES NEW COMMUNITY

Robert Putnam's well-researched book on the collapse of community in America has plagued me since I first read it nearly a decade ago. *Bowling Alone* details the findings of Putnam's research into communal involvement in the United States, telling the story of the dramatic decline in Americans' involvement in political, social, civic, religious and occupational organizations.[6] Putnam's book planted a passion in me to foster stronger and deeper levels of community, whether through my previous position on a church staff, through my current academic studies or through the way my wife and I lead our lives. Developing community among people accustomed to living rather isolated lives has proven to be, at times, rather difficult and incredibly taxing.

It was during a particular low point in my efforts to create community for the people around me that I first read and was deeply encouraged by Michael Welker's *God the Spirit*. One of the most profound points Welker makes in his book is that throughout the events of the Bible, the Spirit of God constantly generated new community.

> In all the early attestations to the experience of God's Spirit, what is initially and immediately at issue is the restoration of an internal order, at least of new commitment, solidarity, and loyalty. The direct result of the descent of God's Spirit is the gathering, the joining together of a people who find themselves in distress. The support of their fellow persons is acquired; a new community, a new commitment is produced. . . .
>
> Even the early experiences of God's Spirit are *experiences of how a new beginning is made toward restoring the community of God's people.* They are *experiences of the forgiveness of sins, of the raising up of the "crushed and oppressed,"* and of the renewal of the *forces of life.*[7]

The Spirit of God creates community out of unlikely situations by using unlikely leaders to call God's people to live in unlikely relationships with each other and with the world. This truth was a profound encouragement and motivation to me as I sought to live like a missionary. I pray it will be the same for you.

Before beginning this session, share your drawings and research from session 4.

Dwelling in the Word

- Begin in prayer, inviting the Spirit to guide your group as you dwell in the text.

- Read aloud Romans 8:1-17.

- After the reading has been completed, allow a few moments of silence to reflect on the passage and what stands out to you.

- Break into pairs (preferably with someone you don't know well) and discuss the following questions. Use this time to practice listening to each other as well as to the text.

- What in the text captured your imagination?
- What question would you most like to ask a biblical scholar?

• Gather once again as a large group and share your partners' responses.

• Review these responses and discuss: What might God be up to in the passage for us today?

Contextual Analysis

In Scripture the Spirit of God created community out of unlikely situations by using unlikely leaders to call God's people to live in unlikely relationships with each other and with the world.

1. How do people experience community (or not) in your local context? What is healthy about the patterns of community involvement? What is less than ideal?

2. If you could change one thing about the way people around you experience community, what would you change?

3. If God chose to change one thing about the way people around you experience community, what do you think he might change?

4. Now think about the Christian communities (including your
   own) in your context. How do you think they reflect (or not) the
   Spirit-led community God desires for his people to be?

Theological Reflection: *The Spirit Who Generates New Community*

5. Break into pairs and consider the following stories of unlikely
   leaders chosen by God to be filled with his Spirit in order to pre-
   serve, restore or generate new community for God's people out of
   unlikely situations. For each person, use the listed text(s) and
   your knowledge about his life to answer the following questions:
   (1) What made him an unlikely leader? (2) How did he form community out of unlikely situations for God's people?

   • Gideon (Judg 6:33-40; 7:15-23); and Jephthah (Judg 11:1–12:7)

   • David (1 Sam 16:1-12; 17:16-54; 2 Sam 7:1-17)

   • Saul/Paul (Acts 9:1-22; 13:1-2)

6. When God's Spirit formed God's people into new community, their community was often defined by unlikely (abnormal, unique, extraordinary) relationships with each other and with the world. Read Ephesians 5:15-21. Now read or skim Ephesians 5:22–6:9, verses which spell out the implications of 5:21. How does the author describe the relationships that take place in a Christian community in these verses?

Missionary Imagination

7. Fill in the blanks:

The primary work of the Spirit of God is to _____ the people of God to _____ in the mission of God and in so doing to _____.

The primary means by which the Spirit _____ God's people is by liberating them from _____ and equipping them with gifts to _____ to the world.

8. How might the Spirit of God need to transform your church/group/faith community into a more Spirit-generated community?

9. What would it look like if God's Spirit were to generate new community in your local context? What might change? How could you participate in that?

10. Identify 2-3 people or groups of people in your local context who you might be able to serve by providing new community for them. What are some steps you might take to help them experience the community that God's Spirit generates?

Before We Meet Again

- Other texts that discuss the change the Spirit brings to the community of God's people include Acts 2:42-47; 4:32-37; Romans 8:1-30; 1 Corinthians 6:9-11; Galatians 5:13-26. Read and reflect on these texts during the week. Search for other passages as well. Record your thoughts and observations here.

- Look back at question 10. Take some steps toward providing community for the people you identified. In the following space, write down what you did and any thoughts or reflections you have from your experience.

- Based on your continued conversations and reflections, modify your one-sentence summary of your current understanding of what it looks like to live by the power of the Spirit (look back to sessions 1-4). Record your new sentence here.

LIVING AS THE CHURCH
IN THE POWER OF THE SPIRIT

An oft-repeated critique of the prevailing model of church in the West is that it produces a passive membership. During the twentieth century, the predominant model for Christian leadership became pastor/teacher—professional clergy tasked with the pastoral care and right teaching of the church. Church members were asked to receive this care and to sit under this teaching. Unfortunately, the model soon gave birth to a system in which professional church leaders provided religious goods and services for members to consume—producing a flurry of activity from a specialized few, but resigned passivity from the masses.

Many voices have called for reformation of that system, including Jürgen Moltmann and Alan Hirsch. Moltmann, a German theologian, argues in *The Church in the Power of the Spirit* that every individual in every local congregation is called to active fellowship with Christ and active service for his kingdom in the power of the Spirit.[8] Moltmann spells out in more than four hundred magisterial pages what it might look like if the church truly grasped that *all* of its members were empowered to participate in the mission of God, rather than deferring the majority of the responsibility to its professional leadership.

Hirsch delivers a similar message in *The Forgotten Ways*, arguing that the Christian church started out as a movement because each individual carried a missional DNA—a sense of ownership of the mission of God.[9] Hirsch believes the church has largely forgotten these ways (hence the title of his book) and calls for the church to become a missional movement once again by awakening the missionary genius in each one of its members.

You may or may not agree with the arguments of Moltmann, Hirsch or others who critique contemporary models of church organization, but hopefully their message for what the church ought to be hits home. Their simple message is this: the church, at its core, is a group of believers who are individually and communally called, gathered, empowered and sent into the world to participate in God's mission.

This session is designed to help you discover how the Spirit has empowered you to participate in God's mission in, through and with your group, church or faith community.

Share your experiences with creating community since the last week.

Dwelling in the Word

- Begin in prayer, inviting the Spirit to guide your group as you dwell in the text.

- Read aloud Romans 8:1-17.

- After the reading has been completed, allow a few moments of silence to reflect on the passage and what stands out to you.

- Break into pairs (preferably with someone you don't know well) and discuss the following questions. Use this time to practice listening to each other as well as to the text.

- What in the text captured your imagination?
- What question would you most like to ask a biblical scholar?
- Gather once again as a large group and share your partners' responses.
- Review these responses and discuss: What might God be up to in the passage for us today?

Contextual Analysis

Look back at your notes from the contextual analysis sections of all the previous weeks. Spend 10-15 minutes reviewing, recapping and summarizing the key discoveries you made during the previous sessions and then answer the following:

1. What type of church/people/group would it take to live on mission in this context?

2. How well do you and your group currently represent the answer from the first question?

Spend some time in prayer before moving on to theological reflection. Ask God to fill you as individuals and as a group with the power of his Spirit so that you might participate in his mission for your local context.

Theological Reflection: *The Spirit Who Empowers the People of God to Participate in the Mission of God*

3. The Spirit empowers the people of God to participate in the mission of God by speaking the words of God and by being witnesses to who God is and what God has done. Each person in your group should read aloud one of the following passages: Isaiah 59:21; 61:1-2; Acts 1:8; 2:1-4; 4:8-20, 23-31; 6:8-15; 7:54-56; 1 John 4:1-6, 13-16. What do you notice?

4. The Spirit also empowers the people of God to participate in the mission of God by building them into the body of Christ, a community gifted to live by the grace of God and bestow that grace on the world. Read Romans 12:3-8, 1 Corinthians 12:12-30 and Ephesians 4:1-16. Based on these texts, what does it mean to be the body of Christ built by the Spirit? Why does the Spirit give gifts to the church?

5. Last, the Spirit empowers the people of God to participate in the mission of God by filling them with the presence of God, allowing them to reveal God's presence to the world. The notion of being filled with the presence of God is a theme of the book of Ephesians

(see Eph 1:23; 2:22; 3:17, 19; 5:18). Read each of these verses. How would you summarize the author's idea of God as present in his people? What is significant about God's presence with his people?

Missionary Imagination

6. Write in your own words how you would answer if someone were to ask you what you think the role of the Spirit is.

Every member of your group is empowered by God's Spirit to be a witness, to serve God's kingdom and God's church, to experience fellowship with God, and to reveal the presence of God to the world. With this truth in mind, follow the following directions.

7. Divide into three groups. Each group will cover one of the three ways the Spirit empowers God's people as discussed in the theological reflection section: witness, gifts and presence.

   • Write a job description specifically for your group based on your assigned power from the Spirit. Write it like a detailed job posting you might find on a company's website.

   • When each of the three groups has finished, share your job descriptions with everyone.

   • Create a common document that details what it looks like for your group to live in the power of the Spirit based on all three job descriptions.

Final Assignments

- Continue to read and reflect on Romans 8:1-17 or any other passage from this week's conversation. Record your thoughts here:

- Organize an event/party for your group that includes food, fellowship, a time to process the highs and lows of the process of working through the conversation guide, and a time to plan and commit to next steps for the group to take.

- It is often said that teaching is the best form of learning. Therefore, identify 2-6 other people in your life who you could take through the material covered during your study or the key learning you gleaned from the conversations. Use this conversation guide or create your own process to take your 2-6 friends through a learning journey with you.

- Based on your continued conversations and reflections, modify your one-sentence summary of your current understanding of what it looks like to live by the power of the Spirit. Record your new sentence here.

TIPS FOR HAVING GREAT SMALL GROUP GATHERINGS

The following tips were gleaned from my experience in small group ministry. Practice these over the course of your time together, but know they are not exhaustive. Space has been left at the end for your group to add its own tips for having great small group gatherings.

TIP 1: *Be Prepared*

Group gatherings flourish when folks come prepared. If there is one person designated to lead or facilitate the gathering, that person should be in prayer throughout the week, asking God's Spirit to lead him or her and to be present at the gathering. The leader or facilitator should also personally work through the material a couple of times so he or she can create a gathering that flows smoothly and achieves the desired objectives.

It is also important for group members to come prepared. Their preparation includes completing midweek assignments, bringing required materials, opening their minds to what God might want to say and opening their lives to where the Spirit might want to lead.

TIP 2: *Foster Habits That Create Good Conversation and Discussion*

There is a reason these guides have been titled Forge Guides for Missional Conversation. They are meant to *create conversation* about living missionally! It is important that groups foster habits that help create good conversation. These habits include:

- Directing discussion toward all group members, not just the facilitator. Often when someone responds to a question, he or she will look at the person who asked the question. Group members should look at and interact with one another while giving their responses, not just the leader.

- Avoid the silent head nod, which is one of the biggest conversation killers. Unfortunately, it is a hard habit to break. However, when someone shares or offers a response, the group should work to give more of a response than the silent nod. Perhaps someone could ask a question, share their own insight, request for the person to say more or even just say thanks.

- Ask good questions and follow-up questions. The questions provided for you in the conversation guides will hopefully be effective at sparking conversations. It is imperative that the group does not merely answer the questions provided but asks new questions as the conversation continues. Asking new questions is a good indication that group members are listening to one another and taking an active interest in what is being said.

- Draw answers out of each participant. One of the cardinal sins of teaching or leading a discussion is to answer your own question to avoid the awkward silence. If a question is asked and no one answers after you have allowed for a comfortable time of silence, consider repeating or rephrasing the question. Also consider calling on a specific person to answer. Most of the time the person called on will have something insightful to share. I often am amazed at what the quietest people in groups have to say when a leader calls on them to specifically share. As a last resort, suggest that the group come back to the question later, or give time for individuals to share with their neighbor before sharing with everyone.

- As much as possible, affirm what others say. People feel affirmed when their thoughts are repeated or referred to later in the discussion. When people feel affirmed, they are more likely to continue to participate in the conversation.

- Clarify or summarize what has been said. Sometimes a group member will offer a long answer or get sidetracked onto a different discussion. It is often helpful for the group leader or another member to summarize what has been said, even asking for clarity if necessary. This clarifying practice will help keep the conversation moving in a focused direction.

TIP 3: *Share Leadership and Always Give People Something to Contribute*

Small groups flourish when all members are given a chance to lead on a regular basis and when all members are expected to contribute to each gathering. Rotate leadership and facilitating responsibilities while working through this guide if at all possible. Always try to find ways to ensure everyone is bringing something to contribute, whether an activity to plan or simply a snack to share.

TIP 4: *Encourage and Affirm One Another as Much as Possible*

A little bit of affirmation goes such a long way in small groups. Telling someone he or she had a good idea, did a good job leading, brought good energy to the group or made a nice snack will encourage the person to continue to participate in group gatherings in important ways. Groups that are able to identify each other's strengths and to encourage those strengths to be used more will be full of life, energy and possibility.

TIP 5: *Create Space for Feedback*

Group gatherings will be better over the long run if the group can create a regular rhythm of giving and receiving feedback about group gatherings. Allowing all members to give input or offer ideas for future gatherings will increase ownership and help craft an experience unique to the group.

RECOMMENDED RESOURCES
FOR FURTHER STUDY

I have had the privilege to teach on all things related to the missional church in a wide variety of settings. It is a common occurrence for me to discover that those who joined me in the learning experience often are only aware of one small portion of the missional church movement. Most folks I meet seem to only have one or two authors or teachers who have encouraged them to think and live more missionally. Consequently, these folks often have only one or two ideas of what it might look like for a Christian or a church to think and live missionally. I always love watching their expressions of surprise and joy when I tell them that the missional church conversation has been going on for over a century and has produced hundreds of books and dozens of different ideas for what the missional church might actually look like in reality. More than anything, though, I love to watch their imaginations grow as they encounter fresh voices and new ideas.

If you would like to broaden your missional imagination even further than you have already done through this study guide, the following resources will help you.

1. "A Brief History of the Missional Church Movement." This short essay describes the growth of the missional church movement from the World Missionary Conference in Edinburgh (1910) through today, identifying a variety of sources that have funded the movement. You can find this essay online at www.ivpress.com.

2. "Helpful Resources for Developing Missional Imagination." This list of resources is given to everyone who plays a leadership role in the Forge Mission Training Network so that they can expand their own imaginations for mission and help others do the same. You can view the list at www.ivpress.com. For more information on the books, you can view my list at www.worldcat.org/profiles/luthercml3/lists/2934221.

Notes

[1]Alan Hirsch, "Defining Missional," *Leadership Journal*, fall 2008, www.christianity today.com/le/2008/fall/17.20.html.

[2]"Dwelling in the Word" is a practice developed and taught to me by Dr. Patrick Keifert of Church Innovations (www.churchinnovations.org). The instructions provided are a slightly modified version of the guide provided in Patrick Keifert and Pat Taylor Ellison, *Dwelling in the Word: A Pocket Handbook* (Minneapolis: Church Innovations Institute, 2011). For more on Dwelling in the Word, visit www.churchinnovations.org/06_about/dwelling.html.

[3]David H. Kelsey, *To Understand God Truly: What's Theological About a Theological School?* (Louisville: Westminster/John Knox Press, 1992).

[4]Michael Welker, *God the Spirit* (Minneapolis: Augsburg Fortress, 1994), p. 127.

[5]Ibid., p. 119.

[6]Robert D. Putnam, *Bowling Alone: The Collapse and Revival of American Community* (New York: Simon & Schuster, 2000).

[7]Welker, *God the Spirit*, pp. 57, 65.

[8]Jürgen Moltmann, *The Church in the Power of the Spirit: A Contribution to Messianic Ecclesiology* (New York: Harper & Row, 1977).

[9]Alan Hirsch, *The Forgotten Ways: Reactivating the Missional Church* (Grand Rapids: Brazos Press, 2006).

Forge Guides
for Missional Conversation

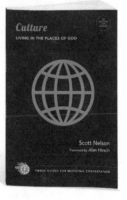

COMMUNITY: *Living as the People of God*
MISSION: *Living for the Purposes of God*
POWER: *Living by the Spirit of God*
VISION: *Living Under the Promises of God*
CULTURE: *Living in the Places of God*

Forge

How can God's people give witness to his kingdom in an increasingly post-Christian culture? How can the church recover its true mission in the face of a world in need? Forge America exists to help birth and nurture the missional church in America and beyond. Books published by InterVarsity Press that bear the Forge imprint will also serve that purpose.

Forge Books from InterVarsity Press

Creating a Missional Culture, JR Woodward

Forge Guides for Missional Conversation (set of five), Scott Nelson

The Missional Quest, Lance Ford and Brad Brisco

More Than Enchanting, Jo Saxton

The Story of God, the Story of Us, Sean Gladding

For more information on Forge America, to apply for a
Forge residency, or to find or start a Forge hub in your area,
visit **www.forgeamerica.com**

For more information about Forge books from
InterVarsity Press, including forthcoming releases,
visit **www.ivpress.com/forge**